A NUANCED PAUSE

Suprabha

INDIA • SINGAPORE • MALAYSIA

ISBN 979-8-89186-855-7

Images used on cover and interior are AI-generated

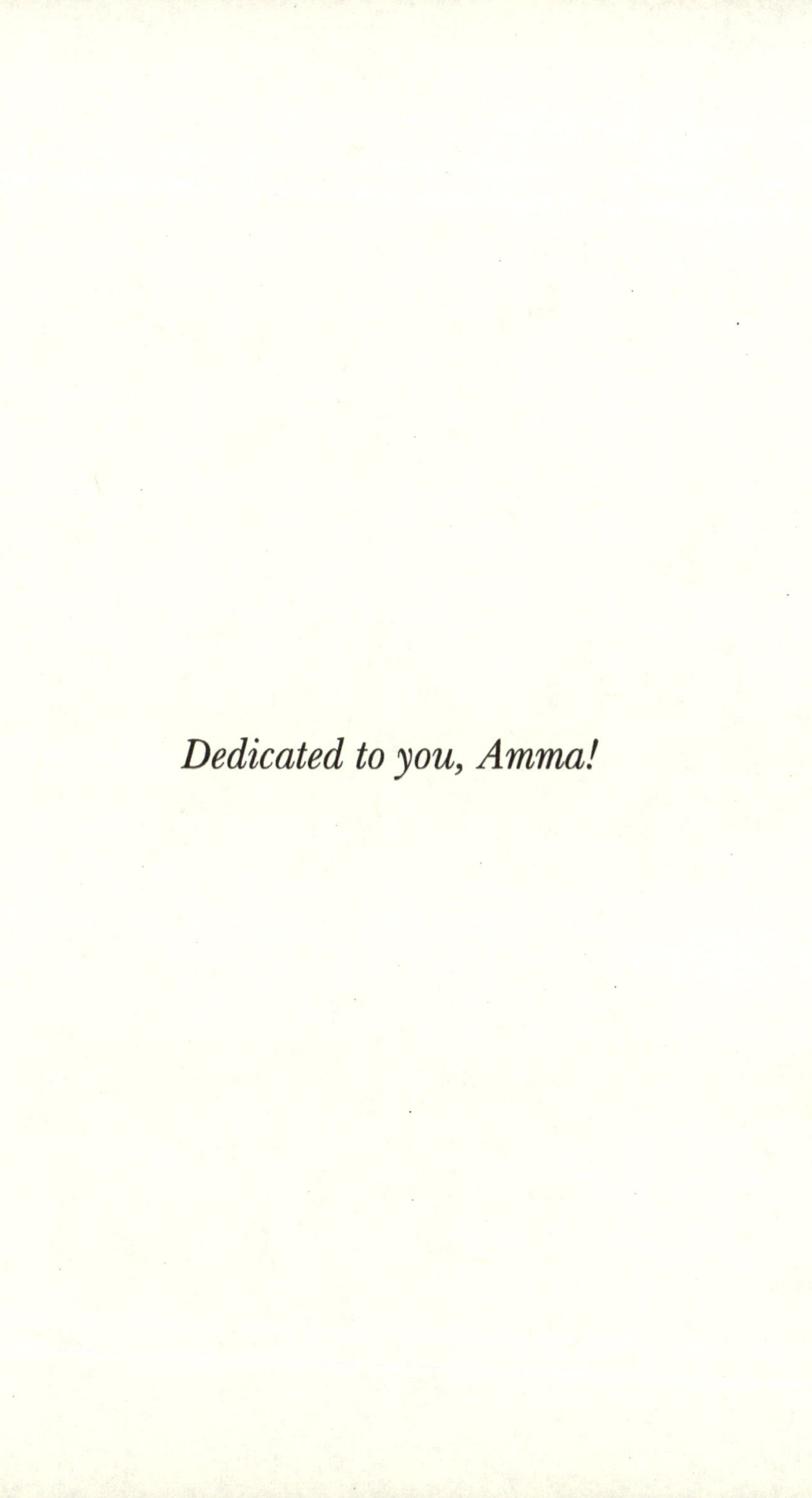

Dedicated to you, Amma!

Contents

Introduction

Kaleidoscope is Life
Every now and then, look back to observe
Changed reality, altered perceptions,
Uncovered revelations, focused memory
Such a wonder is Life!

Two coinciding life events is the genesis of my debut book where I look back at life to string together slivers of memories, relive emotions and reflect on experiences as a means of catharsis. Poems 40 & 41 are symbolic and an ode to Amma (my Mother).

I have curated 51 poems sectioned into 5 factions – Childhood Innocence; Rebellious Youth; Views about the World; Experiments with Love and Experience with Life.

Childhood Innocence talks about significance of birth, early memories and growing up with siblings. A trip down the memory lane to reminisce our favourite moments as a child, experiences at school and early friendships.

Rebellious Youth is a reflection of a typical teen with see-sawing emotions. Since a lot of these were written during my teen, they carry a certain rawness and naïve outlook to life.

Worldly Views reflect perceptions about current state of affairs from a bystander point of view. They are rather a sombre take on the world, questions the idea of reality and dreams of a better tomorrow.

Experiments with Love is a take on relationships and their inherent complex nature. These poems reflect finding oneself through deciphering the intricacies of different types of relationships in a lifetime.

Experience with Life highlights the circle of life with neither a beginning nor an end. They are deep, nuanced and bring forth a certain maturity attained when life happens. The observations question the idea of identity, existence, and spirituality.

I truly hope the poems resonate with you as they relate to the dreams, hope and scars we all carry when we live life.

Wonder Years

Childhood Innocence

Ever notice that when you turn back in time, out of the countless moments, only few standout?

Mediocre feelings are rarely remembered,
chance encounters hardly touch your heart.
only experiences which evoked deep emotions leave an indelible mark.

Every birth carries with it a certain miracle,
a sense of achievement and a true possibility
but it can also be a process,
a sense of duty and a mere statistic.

Learning to put a little distance between ME and MINE – a lesson taught by life but takes a lifetime to master.

Born Here

Born in this body, limited by the physical,
Carefully filtered appearances, curated wounds,
Identifying with emotions fathomed, every reaction justified,
My feelings, my logic, my memories, all are me,
Experience of the being through endless drama.

Born in this society, limited by the identity,
Eager for a faction to belong, inherited traits,
Owning a tribe's legacy, every division warranted,
My name, my status, my entitlements, all are me,
Experience of the being through tireless pursuit.

Born in this planet, limited by the resources,
Incredibly engineered conception, balanced subtly,
Abiding the unwritten laws, every creation matters,
My soil, my water, my climate, all are mine,
Experience of the being through selfless co-existence.

Born in this cosmos, limited by imagination,
Grandiose spectrum of light, infinitely timeless,
Accepting our minuscule presence, every breath conscious,
My soul, my journey, my karma, all are mine,
Experiencing the being through boundless gratitude.

Childhood Reminisces

I remember

Unrecognisable faces after a day with colours, muddy water, glitter, and eggs.

Distinct smell of burnt twinkling stars, dancing circles, roaring triangles, and whistling rockets.

Pretty pandal for a huge idol with stories of an elephant head, a friendly mouse, and the laughing moon.

Toothy smiles before exchanging a basket of sweets, fruits, and a coin or two.

I remember

Looking for the shiniest piece of a broken tile to hop on nine-blocks drawn on the road.

Challenged to sing a song starting with a particular alphabet before the tick of the clock.

Pretend class in half draped saree, borrowed glasses, chalk dust and wide-eyed obedient dolls.

Sunsets spent arranging a pile of flat stones while dodging incessant ball attacks.

I remember

Being picked up after the last of the exams to an unknown wonderland.

Thrown together with a friendly group of travellers never seen before, never to see again.

Crowded stations with blaring horns, hiccupping berths, and fading locales out of the window.

Walking endlessly, playing with the waves, chased by a monkey, and posing in front of monuments.

I remember

Tying up my anklet made from loose bells, perfecting a posture, loose costumes, and young expressions.

Early morning practice of drowsy melody, tracking rhythm with my fingers and being out of tune.

Pasting stamps on a page, hoarding coins in a pouch, searching streets for matchbox covers unique and used.

Being on stage, playing king in a play, serenaded by a boy, waiting backstage and my voice on the mic.

I remember

Opening the lunch box at noon, wafting aromas, colourful rice meals and mom's secret flavours.

Evening ritual of my grandma's veiny hand carrying a cup of brown sugary milk and fried snacks.

Unannounced late-night party of thick mango milkshake, hot spicy plates of street food and an affable uncle.

Heady concoction of tangy tamarind, beaten to pulp, smeared on a stick as lollipop and a determined cousin.

I remember.

School Days

Chapter I Pristine Friendships

You stumble upon a trusted confidant to share your thoughts sans the worldly veil,
Some thoughts end up in joyous cries while others in tearful joy.

Hold on to an unspoken oath of secrecy facing young feelings, new experiences together,
Some experiences result in accidental euphoria while others in covered-up accidents.

Form an unadulterated bond peppered with simplistic fun, honesty, vulnerability,
Some bonds survive life's journey while others are in the memory for life.

Chapter II Innocent Love

You are drawn to the expressive eyes, long floppy hair, an impish half-smile,

Some have a personality to match while others fail to match-up.

Easily impressed by intelligence, a smooth talker, a thinking mind,

Some can make you swoon with their words while other's wordy discourse is beyond you.

Manage to capture a few hearts with your effervescent presence,

Some express their love unabashedly while others loved in silence.

Chapter III Exploring Me

You follow the unwritten rules, practice the given faith out of habit,

Some beliefs speak to your soul directly while others get misdirected.

Willing to try the forbidden, eager to live up to your peers,

Some vices you learn to outgrow while others continue to grow on you.

Tested at every corner to build a character worthy for life,

Some virtues become second nature in no time while others take a lifetime.

Chapter IV Discovering Passion

You are enthralled by passionate teachers, their optimism contagious,

Some make you fall in love with the subject while others make you the subject.

Being silly, good-old wise cracks, scribbled notes and intended pun,

Some made life fun while others were made fun of by life.

Inspired to believe in a future of choice, endless possibilities, all for the taking,

Some chase the promised future while others are chased by their past.

Like No Other

Growing belly builds anticipation in a little life,

Promise of an incoming cuddly baby to hold, to sing, to talk,

Ushered into a sterile white room to peek at the bundle of joy,

Introduced to thick curly hair, blinking pair of eyes, wrapped like a burrito,

A foreign emotion of instant belonging, a precious gift hand-made just for me.

Growing up with siblings mean you are never lone,

A playmate, a roommate, a companion to share your everyday,

From schools to friends, from hand-me-downs to twinning on occasions,

Invariably wanting the same thing, arguing who is loved more, tossing blame,

Silly fights, episodes of silence but always a united front when pulled up.

Growing into one's own family, diverging personalities and conflicting priorities,

Identifying with ego, sense of self takes on a new meaning,

A whole divided into parts, better halves don't necessarily fit together as hoped,

Some hurt leaves a scar, few experiences create a void, destinies may take you afar awhile,

Picking up exactly where you left-off, no love lost, no distance ever matters.

Growing old and orphaned, losing many lives along the journey too,

Strength of the bond grows stronger albeit the incessant blows,

All acquired relationships will eventually run its course,

Learning to show-up for each other despite everything life throws at you,

A strong emotion of unwavering love, a precious gift hand-made just for me.

An Innocent Circus

An ever smiling red-nosed clown in polka dotted shirt waving at me,

Handlebar moustached magician in mid-night cloak brandishing a wand,

I saw, every movement was exaggerated, every trick was unseen before,

I was surrounded by untouched newness, all mine for the taking,

Oh Innocence, How I miss you!

A steely unicycle peddling juggler with neon curly hair throwing balls in the air,

Overtly tall men in stilts walking around like they were born with it,

I felt, every ball was acting on command, every step was defying nature,

I was surrounded by unfolding amazement, element of surprise hidden in all,

Oh Innocence, How I miss you!

Ferocious lions with pruned manes jumping through the hoop,

Gigantic elephants with artistically painted trunks balancing a ball,

I thought, every roar was an appreciation, every whiplash was an encouragement,

I was surrounded by limitless source of joy, idea of fear unheard of,

Oh Innocence, How I miss you!

Lean jelly-limbed acrobat in shiny pink leotard swinging high on a trapeze,

Miniature figured people in cone-shaped hats ricocheting across like a loose canon,

I believed, every fall was destined, every jump was meant to land on the net,

I was surrounded by best intentions, life-centric decisions always,

Oh Innocence, How I miss you!

Fire And Ice

Rebellious Youth

A step on to the threshold of youth unlocks a personality none knew existed. Hijacked by hormones, emotions are naive, experiences are novice and coming to terms with it all overwhelming and daunting.

One moment you are -

Being in love with the idea of love,

Obsessing over an image perfected,

Looking through rose-tinted lens romanticising everything around,

With expectations from life filled with optimism.

Next moment you are –

Being in love with the idea of pain,

Obsessing over all things that need change,

Looking through dark-tinted lens trivialising everything around,

With expectations from life filled with despair.

Life of a teen appears to be an infinite see-saw between glee and angst.

Do You Know Her?

I often wondered what people meant when they said, "Life is a routine"

Must be true, we now do what's expected of us and not what we truly want to do.

Last thing I want to do is go to college, but I am there on the dot

Talk at length with people not knowing their names

Promise to keep in touch when I have no such intentions

Listen to lectures which is proven unusable out in the world

When I finally want to be there, it's past my allotted time.

Back home all I want to do is chill, but I am comprehending my thoughts

Eager to narrate today's saga instead you find me only listening

Pulled into giving opinions when I have none

Listen to raging metal which is proven to be awakening

When I finally want to be there, it's past my allotted space.

In life, I find myself lonely when I badly need company

Give out a brilliant smile though my heart is crying out loud

Burst into tears when I have no valid reasons

Listen to perspectives which is proven to be judgemental

When I finally want to be there, it's past my allotted passion.

I often wondered what people meant when they said, “Life is a routine”

Must be true, we now become what’s expected of us and not what we truly want to be.

Only You

In a room so crowded,
My eyes search for your presence.

In a mood so festive,
My soul is depressed without your bright smile.

In the company of friends so soothing,
My mind is restless without your comforting words.

In the arms so comforting,
My body is aching for your strong embrace.

In a home so familiar,
I'm so lost without you in my life.

In this world so large,
My heart is all empty waiting for you.

Unfulfilled Dream

The world is plunged into darkness,
She comes out clad in a dazzling silver gown,
Peeping through my window, she lights a candle of desire in my heart.

I turn around to find you bathed in the silvery moonlight,
As we stare into each other's eyes through eternity,
The mystery in your mischievous eyes puts the moon to shame.

Adam sings Everything I do in the background,
As I dance in your arms with my head resting on your broad shoulders,
I have no place else to go, I have met my destiny.

The golden rays of the sun stealthily glances into my room,
Catching a smile of satisfaction on my lips, eyes mirroring a saga of unfinished promise,
I realise, patience pays but pains.

You Talking To Me?

You thought you were blessed, thought you were gifted,

Think again, you could not be more wrong,

Between us, I don't know who was first but I'm always there where you are.

Initially you were ignorant about my presence,
I let you sail in that bliss for a while,

I gave you pain, gave you hell,

Now that you know I am here, you have no place else to go.

I have my eyes on you, watching your every move,

You have braved me so far, countered me with devices taught to you by the world,

You think you are smart, let's see who will have the last laugh.

I'm in you, around you, for you and against you,

If you think the future is different, maybe you are right or you couldn't be more wrong,

I fear none other than the door, hoping you will give up and opt out.

One Not-So-Fine Day!

It's a bright sunny day, breeze playing see-saw,

Perfect to lead me to a good mood, happiness came for company too.

My spirits are soaring high, smiles come easily,

Truce is called at home, everybody is at peace, love is humming.

Being one in the heaven of my thoughts, clear as crystal,

Amidst this celebration of life, hope is here with me coaxing me to wait patiently for him.

Ah! What a way to live.

It's a deadly scorching day, heatstroke playing peek-a-boo,

Perfect to push me into an ugly mood, boredom came to play too.

My spirits have hit rock bottom, silly tears waiting to spill,

War is called at the house, everybody is at loggerheads, irritation is singing.

Lost in the hell of my thoughts, hard as a code,

Amidst this mockery of life, desperation is here with me goading me to search frantically for him.

Ah! What a way to exist.

A Painted You

Unleashed in this world you are, are you the one for me? Are you?

I had a glimpse of you in white,
Your aura beckons as you effortlessly make your presence felt.
Like the moon's rays touching the world,
You touched mine and I now see eternal peace in the dusk.

I saw you the other day in yellow,
Your face gleams as you intently gaze afar into the horizon.
Like the sun which brightens the world,
You enlightened my soul, and I said a final goodbye to loneliness.

I met you crossing my path in blue,
Your eyes invite as you dive deeper into mine.
Like the sky which envelops the world,
You embraced me tight, and I know with those arms around me comfort is assured.

I spoke to you yesterday in black,
Your masculinity undeniable as you walked intensely towards a purpose.
Like the animal instinct which rules the world,
You held my hand and I no longer need to worry about my life.

You took my breath away today in red,

Your being ready to be loved as you flash that smile unique to me.

Like the rainbow which spreads magic in the world,

You enchanted my heart and my belief in love is now re-affirmed.

Untethered in this world you are, you are the one for me. You are.

In The Arms Of Summer

The desperate summer is back with a vengeance.

Holding all and sundry in its scorching embrace.

The yellow sun stares right into your eyes,

Challenging you to fight the all-powerful.

The sky has wrapped herself in a blue and white cloak,

Clear as crystal she is hinting your mind to follow suit.

Birds with their wings apart are trying to reach the unreachable,

Asking you to chase your dreams too.

Summer brings along with it a slow pace,
Lethargy is spread rampant everywhere.
As I sit expressing myself again,
Yawning insistently though I am doing what I like best.

It feels like my whole being is at rest,
My mind body and soul are at peace with stress at bay.
In this relaxing bliss, everything seems perfect except my heart,
Wonder why it's so restless; probably it's feeling lonely again.

From Nowhere To Nowhere

In the midst of nowhere it lay,
Happy to be swept by a mirage.

Now hidden in an enclosed hollow,
An object shimmering bright.

Well-guarded and protected it is,
More as a duty than out of love.

Many look from afar sensing cold,
Move onto things warm and fuzzy.

Few dare to touch attracted to aloofness,
Toss it aside fearing it's contagious.

Keen eyes praise the depth and clarity,
Relating to its triumph through trials.

The object lays motionless,
Questioning its very identity.

Is it a diamond found rare?
Or just another stone found everywhere?

Who Am I?

Image is the beholder's collection,
Perception of you through the eyes of others,
Eyes which note only what it wants to see,
Limited by the colours in their palette,
Once stroked, rarely traced over,
Painting a different you.

Image is the owner's showcase,
Impression of you in your own eyes,
Eyes which mirror only what others want to see,
Burdened by the moulds in your satchel,
Once shaped, rarely not remodelled,
Sculpting a different you.

Image is the creator's illusion,
Expression of you in the eyes of all,
Eyes which reflect only what lies beyond to see,
Bound by the spells in the trove,
Once cast, rarely broken
Envisioning a different you.

Wordly Words

Views of the World

Do you wonder about our relationship with the world and our part in it? Do you wonder if we matter in the world or should the world matter to us? How to be in the world yet not be in it?

Enamoured with the world if you are

You see what the world sees and everything you see seem real

You feel what the world feels and everything you feel seem valid

You do what the world does and everything you do seem justified

World begins and ends with you.

Disillusioned with the world if you are

You challenge the perception of the world and everything you see is surreal

You distance your feelings from the world and everything you feel is balanced

You question your actions in the world and everything you do is thoughtful

World begins and ends without you.

Road To Freedom

I dream a dream where the reins of my life are in my hands,

Where I am free to be me,

Where there are none who consider me not one amongst them.

I dream a dream where I sit all day writing my heart out,

Where I am not afraid of mouthing my feelings,

Where there is no scope for tears in my eyes.

I dream a dream where I am surrounded by people who genuinely love me,

Where I am proud of my flaws,

Where there is value for who I am than how I look.

I dream a dream where I am on my way to the ultimate freedom,

Where journey matters as much as the destination,

Where this dream is not just a dream.

World Drying Up?

Drop by drop,
Drop makes an ocean.
Waves roar with delight,
In the abode of sun, it glows,
In the reign of the moon, it gleams.

Seasons come and go,
But rain fails.
Waves no longer roar,
Dawn to dusk the ocean is still,
Earth drying up, so are we,
Drop by Drop.

A Life's Saga

Standing on the threshold of life, armed with innocence,

I opened my eyes to the world searching for love, trust in anyone I met.

Though I cried, it was a cry of joy,

My innocence made me see love all around.

Time, true to its nature flew by, armed with knowledge,

I looked at the world and it's discriminating degree of love.

I cried, not out of joy but pain,

My insecurity made me withdraw from people all around.

Today I have walked the road long enough, armed with no expectations,

I still see the same world now with greater bias, hatred, and mistrust.

I cry no more, none left,

My betrayals made me realise love doesn't exist all around.

As this sad saga continues, armed with experience,

I hope to see a world full of love, happiness, and peace.

I wish to laugh mirthful,

My maturity makes me look for a miracle all around.

Slow Poison

This world is a burning hell,

Bias has set the lives here on fire,

History hasn't taught us anything but to repeat itself,

How can you say life is rosy?

When all I can see is a bed of thorns.

This world is an abode for cruelty,

Right to be born is snatched away based on gender,

A man's life is cut short basis his religion,

How can you say there will be sunshine tomorrow?

When all I can see is an endless night.

This world has lost its sense of purpose,
Justice died long ago when people were given jobs in exchange of favours,
Hands of friendship are extended basis wealth,
How can you say there will be a happy ending?
When all I can see is tragedy.

This world is not what I wish to live in,
Arms of support are lent based on your colour,
Arrows of love are nowhere to be found,
How can you say this too will pass?
When every second is killing me.

What's Real?

There was a dearth of choice with unheard voices,
Now there is freedom to choose with a plethora of options,
Are we more inclusive?

There were few close friends to count on,
Now there are thousands behind a screen,
Are we less lonely?

There was an insatiable want to amass materialistic things,
Now there is abundance of wealthy collections,
Are we more fulfilled?

There was pride in going to ivy institutes to acquire multiple degrees,
Now there are many titles added to the name,
Are we more insightful?

There was an ardent belief in following the traditional practices,
Now there is faith only in whatever works personally,
Are we more tolerant?

There was immense joy in living with big families,
Now there is an innate need to be a nuclear unit,
Are we less cultured?

There was a natural balance of work being part of life,

Now there is a majority of the day spent on work,

Are we more healthy?

There was an unstated status attached to an address,

Now there is residence in famous locations,

Are we more community oriented?

There was only ancient knowledge handed down from generations,

Now there is approved food labelling rampant,

Are we less deficient?

There was a constant urge to rapidly urbanise the rural,

Now there is concrete challenges to the natural resources,

Are we more caring?

There was a dream to own a house,
Now there is residence in enviable mansions,
Are we more at home?

There was an effort to improve longevity of life,
Now there is proof of living a long life,
Are we more conscious?

There was million years spent on evolution into human,
Now there is an evolved being high up
in the thought-chain,
Are we more enlightened?

Nature In Its Full Glory

Heralded by a day with most light, brightness for all to witness,

Soaring temperatures, an obscure pond inching away to dry,

Flora has a growth spurt around; mangoes arrive in style.

It's time to nourish yourself, weed out the distractions,

You persist and you protect that dream.

Ushered by the noisy clouds, rain for all to witness,

An occasional rainbow, an obscure pond fills up to it's brim,

Scoops of green added around, leaves unfurl to show-off.

It's time to rejuvenate yourself, take stock of the abundance,

You sustain and you hope for that dream.

Signalled by equal light or dark, gentle breeze for all to witness,

A clear white moon, an obscure pond settles down to clear-up,

Trees begin to shed leaves around; insects plan to leave town.

It's time to accept yourself, reap from the efforts sown,

You move-on and you dare to dream anew.

Announced by the longest night, fog for all to witness,

Random burst of snowflakes, an obscure pond threatens to freeze over,

Vegetation is in slow motion around; animals cosy up to hibernate.

It's time to prepare yourself, balance out the inventory to replenish,

You learn and you give direction to that dream.

Accompanied by longer days, light blue sky
for all to witness,

Confused shifting weather, an obscure pond
turns into ugly green soup,

Flowers blossom with new leaves around,
birds chirp a brand-new song.

It's time to exert yourself, start afresh to
transform,

You act and you fulfil that dream.

Got to Love LOVE

Experiments with Love

If it all begins with "I" and ends with "I", then what is the significance of engaging in so many relationships in your lifetime? Maybe it is to serve an innate need of a social being or maybe it is to serve as a lesson.

In our repertoire of relationships, only few pass the test of time and heart takes note.

Search for the "One" makes the list for most.

From waiting to attraction, attraction to commitment, commitment to heartbreak, heartbreak to let-go, moving-on to starting anew.

The myriad stages of relationships and wordy statuses

Many with fancy names and few best left label-less

Beauty lies always in the journey even if the destination is a heartbreak.

Search for "Self" is rarely explored to its limit.

Sense of self going through the ebb and flow in tune with relationships. Vested too much in others rather than with oneself although we all know which one lasts longer. Hard to come to realisation that relationships mirror dominant emotions and seek to mimic childhood's unfulfilled needs.

Search for "Legacy" is a given and hardly questioned.

Many thoughtlessly bring a life into the world but not many put thought into becoming parents. A sense of accomplishment hard to dismiss and carries with it long-lasting impact. Journey to motherhood for a woman is full of surprises and sacrifices. Every story is unique; every story is valid and every story matters.

Nowhere Yet Somewhere

Sharing thoughts with a faceless you,
A stranger yet a heart mate.
Strange are the ways of the heart,
Weird to the mind yet meaningful.

Living scenes of other's life with a nameless you,
Hallucination yet life like.
Dream is the work of the mind,
Unfulfilling yet promising.

Loving the idea of loving you,
Nobody yet somebody.
Love is the essence of life,
Truth yet rare.

Sometimes

Time sometimes plays games,

Comprehending reality sometimes seem beyond comprehension,

Heart and mind sometimes heartily battle to coexist,

Peace sometime fails to broker peace.

Senses sometimes greedily plan for the future,

Envying happiness sometimes justify being envious,

Lust for love sometimes loves lustily,

Sins of the past sometimes pays sinfully in the present.

Hope sometimes hopes to get a glimpse of you,
Desperation sometimes is not desperate enough,
Taking steps to find you is sometimes a step in itself,
Cannot sometimes believe in the belief of destiny.

Dawn sometimes fails to crack a dawn in my life,
Shadows of grief sometimes shadow my night,
Changes with change is sometimes negligible,
Dream to dream you into life is sometimes a dream.

Sometimes solving life's puzzle is a puzzle.

None Have A Clue

Deep down the blue is the residence of amazement,

Walking on the soft sand leaving behind traces for the foam,

I spot an oyster shell, a possibility hidden within,

Reminiscing about your eyes, an inlet to your thoughts, your world.

Closed shell stores a treasure to be revealed,

Raising my curiosity to know what promises they hold,

I desperately wish to be part of the whirlpool,

Hoping quietly, you open your eyes to let me in.

Open shell shows off it's precious pearl to the world,
Beckoning me to dive headlong throwing caution to the wind,
I oscillate between familiar fear and foreign valour,
Teasing me are your eyes with their sly smiles, smug glint.

The way you look at me renders me speechless,
Sharing secrets known only to the eyes,
I bravely summon you to close this distance between them,
Tempting you are my eyes to put an end to this sweet misery.

A tale unfolds between the eyes, in a crowd where none have the slightest clue.

Yet Again

This life has ceased to be a bundle of surprise,
I'm drained, completely so,
I hoped at least this illusion will turn real,
But my hope is wronged, shattered yet again.

My mind spoke to my heart a thousand times,
My heart had a mind of its own,
Though cautious and slow at first, soon picked up speed,
Now my heart is defeated, smashed yet again.

You crossed over this stone-wall,
Only to turn your back against it,
You are going to be remembered for a long time,
Though my soul is torn, bleeding yet again.

I can see the cracks, but you insist everything seems fine,
Not surprised to see things fall apart,
You will soon turn into somebody I used to know,
Now I am left stranded, alone yet again.

Losing Hope in Hope

You walk alone with no end, the road is enveloped in darkness,

He then walks by and points you to the direction of light.

You stop in the middle of the road, unable to decide which way to go,

He then holds your hand and tells you not to be frightened of the stony path.

You encounter the ups and buckle, seems like a mission impossible,

He then steadies you and the ups have gone unnoticed with his support.

You see the downs and turn back, afraid you may trip and fall,

He then turns you around and with his strong arms you sail your way down.

You hurt by all the meanness around, want to be alone and do nothing but cry,

He then gives a shoulder to lean on and tears will soon be replaced by smiles.

You feel like you're on top of the world, want to shout it out loud to all,

He then looks at you and happiness in his eyes mean more than the world to you.

You usually do not mouth your thoughts, feelings go unexpressed,

He then casually enquires about your day, and you pour out the story from dawn to dusk.

You know he is worth the risk; life would never be the same without him,

He then labels you a friend and your heart forever will carry a tear.

I Know You Will Take Time

An Imagination if you were,
My instincts would have been unstirred.
But a stranger you are,
You will take your time.

A Stranger if you were,
My eyes would have been dry.
But an acquaintance you are,
You will take your time.

An Acquaintance if you were,
My sleep would have been dreamless.
But a companion you are,
You will take your time.

A Companion if you were,
My mind would have been without hope.
But a friend you are,
You will take your time.

A Friend if you were,
My soul would have been peaceful.
But a soulmate you are,
You will take your time.

A Soulmate if you were,
My heart would have been loved.
But a person above all these you are,
You will take your time.

A Thought, A Moment

The sky is a riot of mysterious colours,
He then peaks through his hiding,
Incessant chirping, creeping brightness stirs me,
A unique moment, an unread page awaits.

The day is systematically following the routine,
One more mindless step in the long road ahead,
Enthusiasm and gratitude are companions,
A thought, a moment stalks me,
With you nowhere, my heart stops smiling.

The sky is a romantic's dream come true,
She sits high on the throne of beauty,
Incoherent whispers, soothing tranquility enthrals me,
A lived day, a puzzle solved.

The night is religiously balancing the highs and lows,
One more lapsed step towards the known exit ahead,
Content and hope are friends,
A thought, a moment haunts me,
With you nowhere, my heart is lonely.

Thoughts of you dot my day and night,
My heart is so empty it's hard to carry.

Story Behind The Love Story

The wind whispers, the trees sway,
A faint moonlight and the slightest drizzle,
As we sit amidst nature, we realise,
It's going to be a long night with spoken silence.

I reserve the best wish always for you,
My feelings seek validation only from you,
You are my first choice to laugh with or cry to,
Dawn to dusk in a jiffy just with your presence.

You are stunned by my ability to see through you,
Your walls come down and you let me in,
You have an innate need to protect and secure me,
Dusk to dawn in a jiffy just in my thoughts.

Tonight, we sit to chat in silence,
Questions in our eyes seek answers desperately,
It's an age-old battle between the hearts and minds,
Existence of love is still an unsolved riddle.

Should love be seen or felt?
Spoken or heard? affirmed or assumed?
Know-it-all mind is on its logical trip again,
Torn heart tries to hold its ground in this barrage of questions.

The wind blows, the trees shake violently,
Pitch darkness and heavy rain,
As we sit amidst nature, we realise,
It's going to be a long night with silent words.

But How Do I?

My day begins with the sunlight,
Your unseen presence wakes me,
How do I stop the day?

My eyes find you in every little thing,
Your lively eyes brighten me,
How do I stop seeing?

My lips smile at the thought of you,
Your simple smile cheers me,
How do I stop smiling?

My words are tainted with your talk,
Your unspoken words soothe me,
How do I stop listening?

My heart cries when it senses you are sad,
Your unexpressed emotions haunt me,
How do I stop sensing?

My mind invents reasons to think of you,
Your thoughtless ideas make sense to me,
How do I stop thinking?

My night ends with your dreams,
Your known absence leaves me lonely,
How do I stop dreaming?

My world desires to be a part of yours,
Your plain refusal breaks me,
How do I stop living?

I revolve around you,
Your unjustified pretence ignores me,
How do I stop being me?

In This Lifetime!

Billion seconds tick by,
Only a few we notice,
All my seconds are noticed,
Since the second I saw you.

Million moments pass by,
Only a few we remember,
All my moments are remembered,
Since the moment I met you.

Thousands of hours clock by,
Only a few we appreciate,
All my hours are appreciated,
Since the hour I befriended you,

Hundreds of days roll by,
Only a few we love,
All my days are loved,
Since the day I loved you.

Tens of years cross by,
Only a few we cherish,
All my years are cherished,
Since the year I married you.

Many lives fly by,
Only one we hold true,
All my life is true,
Since this life I lived with you.

Today

Sitting under the moon, pale halo around me,
Breeze playing with my loose curls,
Silently I unlock the door, overlapping thoughts,
Finding my way right now seems quiet tough,
Don't know how to handle a talking heart
and a silent mouth.
But today, I feel like sharing.

Walking with the rain, smell of mud entices me,
Drops sliding past my delicate lips,
Gently I enter through the door, inexperienced emotions,
Searching answers right now seems quite rough,
Don't know how to handle a lonely heart
and a logical mind.
But today, I feel like being in company.

Standing under a banyan tree, aimless trunks surround me,

Wind humming a melody in my ear,

Slowly I sense the walls closing in, paralysed hope,

Hunting reasons to console right now seems quite hard,

Don't know how to handle a lost heart

and a promising destiny.

But today, I feel like dreaming.

Wading against the waves, jelly sand beneath me,

Salty water kissing my gentle face,

Swiftly I reach the locked door, incomplete dreams,

Waiting for opportunities right now seems quite naïve,

Don't know how to handle a hurting heart

and a long journey.

But today, I feel like smiling.

Slipping Away

Silence of the trees, abruptness of the wind,
Sunset on the horizon,
Have the colours faded?

Stale jokes rewind, stories lack lustre,
Humour senses shallowness,
Has the fun stopped?

Bodies reek familiarity, touch demands spark,
Attraction seeks anew,
Has the intimacy fizzled?

Talk camouflages jibes, distance brings peace,
Interests miss commonality,
Have the paths separated?

Old vices surface, suppressed thoughts emerge,
Confused emotions on the rise,
Has the faith departed?

Fresh tears appear, fake smiles hide,
Trust pretends to trust,
Has the love eloped?

Eyes refuse to see, beings fail to respond,
Ache in the hearts grow,
Has the relationship collapsed?

A Bond Beyond Time

Countless faces pass you by,
All blurred and out of focus.
With a seemingly random yet orchestrated event,
A face unseen before, tugs a chord familiar.

Exchanging pleasantries turn into swapping stories,
Meeting by chance turn into planned outings.
Connecting at a speed as if making up for lost time,
Something from the past seem unfinished.

Both were already starring in different stories,
A chosen path, a said life, a present to live.
Realising a missing piece, though not part of the original,
Something in the present is undeniably incomplete.

Expressing new emotion turn into refusing to acknowledge,
Hope of togetherness turn into creating distance.
Living in a society conditioned to label,
Something in the present will remain unsaid.

Years roll, both have played their said part,

Reaching out with anticipation, to keep a promise never made.

Too late for one, time has played it's trick again,

Something for the future seems reserved.

Ready For A Ride?

Relationship like a roller coaster, an irrefutable promise of thrill.

Begins with a spark ignited by a brief interaction,

Prominent awkwardness leads to calculated actions,

Patience is at its peak, genuine interest in the other.

The insufferable teen in you fuels the curiosity to explore,

Talking incessantly about everything and nothing in particular,

Mention of the new-found, colours your conversation.

Every moment together brings glee,

Every moment apart brings memories of togetherness.

Relationship like a roller coaster gathers speed, eager to ride the highs.

Heightened compatibility stimulates a thought of togetherness,

Relaxed stance results in natural misstep in action,

Belief in longevity blinds obvious differences between.

The adult in you celebrates childish acts of affection,

Talking mostly in particular and hardly about nothing,

Re-living scenes of the new-found, dominates your conversation.

Every moment together brings hope,

Every moment apart brings yearning.

Relationship like a roller coaster, quivers at the descent.

Obvious differences threaten to crack the foundation,

Familiarity breeds selfish actions,

Routine permeates in every facet of the relationship.

The intolerant child in you rebels at the trivial,

Talking is obligatory and often uninitiated,

Preferred silence about the old bond, towers your conversation.

Every moment together brings indifference,

Every moment apart brings nonchalance.

Relationship like a roller coster halts, while the next ride beckons.

The Waiting Game

Sky truly is an artist's muse, canvas stretch beyond his view,
Look at that splendid hue of colours, icy blue sewn with swatches of cotton white.

A lone Kite perching on a branch takes flight,
Alert vision and following a trance path,
Swirling around the territory, branding it its own.

Sky truly is a musician's nemesis, sound exists beyond her frequency,
Look at that splendid hue of colours, purple-pink tie-dyed with tangerine yellow.

A lone Kite flying with its majestic wings spread wide,
Soars high trying to touch the sky,
Spirals down out of control, faking its own death.

Sky truly is a magician's trick, illusion prevails beyond his spell,
Look at that splendid hue of colours, glittering grey crocheted with peacock blue.

A lone Me navigating through life can see paradise at arms length,
Lean in to reach and obstructed with unknowns,
Hand still stretched, tear in one eye and smile in the other.

A Silent Wail

I covered a thousand miles,
With faith in my decisions and least regret,
Depositing my trust in life, only present mattered,
One confident step after another, abandoning things based on mind's logic,
Not a moment spared on it as an afterthought.

Invalidated thought creeps in when no one sees,
Talks its way into the unfamiliar reality,
Undeserving gift of two rare seeds, all past pardoned,
I take a step gingerly, careful not to attach emotions,
Only a few allowed moments spent on them.

The seeds true to their nature grow life,
Takes all in its flow with a care for none,
Kindling an unshakeable desire, the future mapped,
I walk at a steady pace, heart quickly overruling the mind,
All moments pledged voluntarily to them.

The young sprouts start to disappear into oblivion,
Slices and scar their way out,
Obvious guilt encompasses, past revisited,
I run in every direction, to be swallowed by the darkness,
Not a moment granted to spend with them.

I embark a new journey of a thousand miles,

With self doubt and blind belief in others wisdom,

Hoping to see acceptance in the eyes of beloved, only future matters,

I stand still, deserted by my heart and mind,

Moment replaced by a moment.

Lullaby To Mine

Take my hand
Let me take you to the land of wonder
Where the angel of the night is waiting for you
Dressed in white she smiles affectionately
So, close your pretty eyes now and say a little prayer.

Take my hand
Let me take you to the house of glitter
Where fairies play their game of patterns
All true hearted wishes do come true
So, close your pretty eyes now and say a little prayer.

Take my hand

Let me take you to the seat of imagination

Where countless woolly ball of yarns jumps through the hoop

A brand-new day with possibilities is in the works

So, close your pretty eyes now and say a little prayer.

Take my hand

Let me take you to the abode of dreams

Where everything beautiful welcomes you

Love all around paradise beckons

So, close your pretty eyes and say a little prayer.

How I wish

In the company of myself I stand,
Content with my choices and accepting the consequences,
Playing with Sia our favourite game,
How I wish I could dream a dream.

In the throes of passion I rise,
Pursuing to find myself and unlocking the possibility,
Dressing up Sia in our favourite overalls,
How I wish I could dream a dream.

In the arms of joy I live,
Laughing with life and not at it,
Narrating Sia a story from our favourite book,
How I wish I could dream a dream.

In the circle of love I thrive,
Love within radiating and enveloping the doubtful,
Rocking Sia to sleep in our favourite chair,
How I wish I could dream a dream.

You too are a Parent

Tiny fingers and wriggling toes, delivered into this world,

A child dots on you, the child is determined to forge a path.

You open your heart to the child adopted,

You orchestrate the best environment, teach through life examples.

Rooted in love, nurturing the inevitable growth,

Yes, you too!

Four paws and animated eyes, accepted you as a master,

A pet puts you on a pedestal, the pet is a selfless giver.

You open your home to the pet brought in,

You setup a routine, draw boundaries through actions.

Rooted in care, keeping company constantly,

Yes, you too!

Fragile mind and frail body, surprised you by reversed roles,

An aged parent forgoes vanity, the aged parent is helpless.

You open your mind to accept the aged person's predicament,

You take care of the needs, build trust through patience.

Rooted in compassion, willingly taking on the responsibility,

Yes, you too!

Shape-shifting idea and grand dream, manifested by your thoughts,

A start-up company tests your limits, the start-up is ever demanding.

You open your vision to bring the start-up to fruition,

You carve-out time from family, deliver results through resilience.

Rooted in passion, directing the route,

Yes, you too are a parent!

Omnipresent and unseen by most, discerned by your perception,

A social cause is steeped in inequality, the cause is never satiated.

You open your perspective to address the cause,

You form a community, drive change through commitment.

Rooted in altruism, thinking beyond oneself,

Yes, you too!

Pristine and the ultimate truth, ingrained in your being,

A soul is in eternal pursuit, the soul is a limitless possibility.

You open your narrow beliefs to achieve soul enlightenment,

You seek a spiritual lead, make progress through practice.

Rooted in faith, taking lifetimes to traverse,

Yes, you too!

Did I Ever Tell You?

You grew up in an old brick house bursting in its seam,

With far too less to expend, many hands stretched out.

Drawing water from a well; grinding with a giant mortar-pestle; movie escapades with a neighbour,

Your stories reflected simple living, hard work and humility.

Did I ever tell you mom?

I learnt to believe in abundance through your story.

You abandoned childhood to play a dotting sister to siblings of gradient ages,

With archaic societies, a girl's right to dream always questioned.

Writing for an astrologer; rolling out countless flat breads; chattering away until wee hours with your inseparable friend,

Your stories reflected perseverance, dignity, and a sense of duty.

Did I ever tell you mom?

I learnt to let myself dream big through your story.

You entered young into a workplace lasting an entire service time,

With pride in your step, bunch of colleagues soon turned thick friends.

Continuously learning; keeping up with change; climbing up the ladder,

Your stories reflected loyalty, finding identity, and standing one's ground.

Did I ever tell you mom?

I learnt to lead through your story.

You agreed to an arranged marriage to herald a new journey,

With added large families, keeping the thread to the old intact.

Turning the house into a cosy home; speeding away on a scooter; buying that first fancy appliance,

Your stories reflected grit, a balancing act, and resilience.

Did I ever tell you mom?

I learnt to strive for mental stability through your story.

You welcomed motherhood to bring three into this world,

With newer responsibilities, determined to provide what you lacked.

Celebrating festivals with fervour; rushing to buy school supplies; planning holidays,

Your stories reflected family, breaking generational cycle and brutal honesty.

Did I ever tell you mom?

I learnt to value personal integrity through your story.

You graduated to be a grandparent, effortlessly nurturing the little ones,

With unparalleled joy, supporting the newness with tested practices.

Massaging a squealing baby; humming a native lullaby; watching the same song-dance sequence for the umpteenth time,

Your stories reflected patience, reliving youth at a slower pace, and passing on traditions.

Did I ever tell you mom?

I learnt to appreciate the importance of expressing love through your story.

You retired after decades of service into an unknown unsettling phase,

With touring different countries, dealing with loss of loved ones.

Early morning walk to the park; organising kitty party games; thrill of stock market wins,

Your stories reflected self reliance, finding purpose and being society conscious.

Did I ever tell you mom?

I learnt to take time to explore passion through your story.

You slipped away into oblivion, shocking yourself and everyone around,

With dwindling faith, losing your confidence, sense of self.

Talking of you in past tense; seeing you only in pictures; missing you,

Your stories reflect a full life, warrior strength and a generous heart.

Did I ever tell you mom?

I learnt to channel crisis to find peace through your story.

A Year Gone By

It was October, muggy and wet,
A mood so gloomy being forced into turning a year older,
Sometimes, a telling instinct brings way more remorse than reality,
A loved one slipped away into oblivion,
So quickly that she forgot to wish me.

It was November, houses adorned with lights,
A numbness engulfs me as we do what we are told by those in the know,
Sometimes, pain of your near ones bring way more pain than your own,
A home for decades is turning into a house,
So quietly that it is noticeable by none.

It was December, melody of carols carried by the wind,

A strange need in me to turn a blind eye to the erupting emotions,

Sometimes, smiles of colleagues bring way more satisfaction than your own smile,

A message from an old friend sparks a memory,

So lost that it's hard to believe those pages of life.

It was January, cheer of the new year still lingered,

A sense of rage brewing within me fuelled by all things around,

Sometimes, anger towards others bring way more solace than at self,

A new challenge is taken on at work,

So interesting that you overindulge to overcompensate.

It was March, another year to a beautiful marriage,

A feeling of melancholy while I received a certificate well deserved,

Sometimes, achievement shared with others bring way more pride than shared with none,

A low-key celebration of your only parent's seventieth,

So child-like that you compete with scurrying tiny tots at paintball.

It was May, mothers are treated like a queen for a day,

A burst of joy to see my little niece trying to act like an adult,

Sometimes, growth of others bring way more satisfaction than your own growth,

A family outing to an exotic string of islands far away,

So pristine that you are mesmerised by the life unseen above water.

It was July, a certain country burst fireworks on the fourth,

A strong urge in me to withdraw from the world at large,

Sometimes, spending time with others bring way more aloofness than time alone,

A business meeting to a country with one of the seven wonders,

So massive that you are amazed at how small you are.

It was September, little kids do love Krishna's birthday,

A wave of tranquility embraces me from within,

Sometimes, keeping traditions alive bring way more closeness than without,

A seed of an idea begins to take form,

So passionate that you are determined to bring it to fruition.

It was October again, muggy and wet,

A mood so gloomy being forced into turning a year older,

Sometimes, taking time to heal brings way more acceptance of the loss,

A loved one is remembered fondly now in old videos and photos,

So serene that you know she will wish you well always.

Circle of Life

Experience with Life

What's LIFE you ask? Not many have figured this out.

There are stories, there are theories and there are beliefs.

Only the person living gets to choose how to truly experience it.

Circle of senses

Receive through the elements; Respond to the stimulation.

Circle of emotions

Feel the feelings; React to the drama.

Circle of actions

Create the cause; Deal with the consequences.

Circle of evolution

Take years to create; Witness the changes.

Circle of life

Born for retribution; Die for continuance.

An Attempt

My mind carries a burdening bundle of thoughts,
Fleeting glimpses of a thought I see at times,
Open one door and meet emptiness,
Try another, find it locked.

My mind is lost in this maze of mirroring thoughts,
Focus abandons me and I am rendered unarmed,
Clearing the fog with the back of my arm,
Purpose used to be here, now obscure.

My mind is naked in this jungle of thoughts,
Cannot think of anything to think anymore,
Aim at one and shoot another,
Sprout of a new feeling betrays my conduct.

I am at the verge of despair, depression circling the site,
Want to wake up from this dreadful nightmare,
Hope imagination finds it's way back,
My mind wants to fly freely in this sky of thoughts.

If Only

If only eyes were blind,
Could have seen no variation in love.

If only tears could spill,
Could have freed myself from this heavy burden.

If only smiles were real,
Could have fooled them behind the false façade.

If only I could talk,
Could have spoken the love I feel.

If only heart was bereft of emotions,
Could have felt like I belonged.

If only love was around,
Could have helped myself to some.

If only there was a choice,
Could have anyway done the right thing.

If only I was weak,
Could have promptly opted to exit.

Then Why?

Eyes of others sparkle brightly
Then why do my eyes fail to glow?

Lips of others smile limitlessly
Then why do my lips refuse to curl?

Minds of others spin dreams boundlessly
Then why does my mind conjure only nightmares?

Thoughts of others think of renewing bonds unabashedly
Then why do my thoughts find solace in loneliness?

Emotions of others albeit unwarranted are expressed freely

Then why do my emotions battle to be acknowledged?

Souls of others rekindle hope instantly

Then why does my soul hold on to despair?

Hearts of others flutter aloud joyfully

Then why does my heart prefer to weep in silence?

Two In One

The smell of mud captures my senses,
Clouds rumble and down comes the rain,
Under the heavy curtain I stand,
Spirits dampened and mood blue.

Look up to find the sun smiling,
In the midst of a downpour, brightness prevails,
Under the umbrella of light I stand,
Heart singing and hope reaffirmed.

The seven-lane road adorns the blue skies,
Duality in nature is what it represents,
Under the colourful arc I stand,
Emotions raw and faith intact.

Desire for closeness alters a relation's fabric,
Being possessive kills little joy in togetherness,
Under the spell of unknown I stand,
Naïve feelings and unsaid promises

When one feels happy and sad at the same instant,
Words become just a string of letters.

A Glimpse Of Life

A story hand-made for you,

Revealed one page a day.

Fully immersed, every high ecstatic, every low desolate,

Turning pages, the story becomes mundane,

A few accept, many turn indifferent,

Now existing without an afterthought,
until the pages run out.

A play screened at large,
Written one scene after another.
Fully energised, every plot a possibility, every twist an opportunity,
Rolling scenes, the play becomes insatiable,
A few ace, many settle on the sideline,
Now surviving without a regret, until the scenes fade out.

A saga chronicled for centuries,
Narrated one book at a time.
Fully aware, every beginning a payback, every pause a recollection,
Flipping books, the saga becomes everlasting,
A few enlighten, many left behind to aspire,
Now living without a boundary, until the books balance out.

Eye See

Naked eyes see the waves,
Ebbing and flowing in an endless rhythm.

Eyes of anger feel the heat,
Blinding the moment and awaiting change.

Eyes with desire look beyond the horizon,
Indifference and disregard for the present abound.

Eyes with insight observe the clear blue,
Calmness and tranquility in the still movements.

Eyes of experience absorb the living,
Shock and awe at face-value.

Eyes of hope appreciate the wonder,
Beauty in every ugliness around

Need Of The Hour

Interesting activity in the hourglass,
Sand free flows with a care for none.

Time like sand slips away,
Replacing moments with moments.

Time was not on time earlier,
Catching up for all the lost time now.

Sand like time seems hard to grasp,
Appearing where you least expect.

Both have stood the test of time,
Answering the questions one dare not ask.

Time was too spacious then,
Now it is not accommodating enough.

Lonely I was, when I hoped time to tick fast,
Alone I am, wishing time to stand still.

They say, “live in the moment”,
True, I want to live in this moment forever.

A Sinking Sailor

Leaving the comfort of the port,
She is forced to sail towards a known end,
Amidst contrast she dwells,
Scorching sun above and cool water below.

Reaching the middle of nowhere,
She is doomed to carry on the pursuit,
Path on either side look similar,
Marching on-course and still lost.

Amazement died an early death,
A sole captain celebrates his loneliness with the crowd,
Cheering milestones of no significance,
Highs fall flat and lows lack depth.

Familiarity gives up and pretence gives in,
Emptiness chokes his heart, his life,
Cruising through his ocean of tears he vows,
Last one to go down and with a smile.

Just An Everyday Drama

The stage is set for the perfect show,
Scenes so rehearsed, it's now second nature,
A one-woman act meant for none.
Audience is clueless and so is the artist,
Both believing what's on display.

Incessant chatter of two small birds on the windowsill,
Brightness spills everywhere uncontrollably and without a care,
Mood perks up mirroring the brightness around.
She sits alone, gazing nowhere,
A residue of a smile still playing on her lips.

And scene.

Relentless pick and drop by a lone bird on a branch high,

Palm trees at a distance sway gently to the afternoon wind,

Mood which spin dreams of togetherness, of success, of eternity.

She sits alone, observing nothing,

Trying to board the plane of dreams too.

And scene.

Cross-over of a group of white birds in an arrow shaped formation,

Ombré hue indescribable, right for the romantics and brave hearts,

Mood melancholy, dreams seem beyond reach, unrealistic, not her.

She sits alone, sensing naught,

Hoping to get a glimpse of the smile lost.

And scene.

Sporadic hoot of an unseen bird fades into oblivion,

Darkness takes reign, crescent moon and glimmer of the stars exist only for contrast,

Mood somber, hope is exhausted by the day's events and ready to retire.

She sits alone, eyes shut,

Wishing for a better scene tomorrow.

And scene.

Life As We Know It

An old play staged again, swimming ahead of a lot,

Born by chance, are we? Free but hinged, are we?

Time trickles, unlearning to learn anew the same old, the same old,

Stages roll, following a new path already laid by a million previously,

Distance expands, finding meaning in bonds that won't tag along the last run,

Spaces shrink, amassing things we know we can't carry beyond,

Lifetime lost, swinging between fear & chasing happiness,

Everything halts as metered,

Is this life as we know it?

A play of light incredible, chosen amidst a pattern,

Born by design, are we? Hinged but free, are we?

Time speeds, learning to unlearn the new & remember the old,

Stages await, discovering an old path half done last time around,

Distance collapse, finding meaning only in the bond which out-runs time,

Spaces enlarge, embracing everything as one & carry none beyond,

Lifetime spent, knowing the known, fear abate, happiness abound,

Everything halts as metered,

Is this life as we know it?

www.ingramcontent.com/pod-product-compliance
Lightning Source LLC
LaVergne TN
LVHW091048150826
845673LV00002B/503